Flags and Banners of the Third Reich

A. S. Walker

R. G. Hickox

C. Farlowe

ALMARK PUBLISHING CO. LTD

First published – November 1973

ISBN 0 85524 151 9 (hard cover edition)
ISBN 0 85524 152 7 (paper covered edition)

Printed in Great Britain by
Silver End Press, Letterpress Division of E. T. Heron & Co. Ltd,
Essex and London, for the publishers, Almark Publishing Co. Ltd,
49 Malden Way, New Malden, Surrey KT3 6EA

Introduction

THIS book aims to provide a general guide to a subject which can create confusion to those approaching it for the first time. The proliferation of flags, uniforms, insignia and similar paraphernalia during the relatively short-lived period of the Third Reich (1933–1945) provides an area of study of great complexity. Over the last few years a large number of works have appeared dealing, in many cases in great depth, with the insignia, badges, decorations and awards, edged weapons, uniforms and equipment of both the armed forces and a number of political organisations. To date, however, no such work has considered—other than in passing—the varieties and types of the Colours of these organisations. It is, therefore, not surprising that both the modeller and collector alike may have, until now, experienced some not inconsiderable difficulty in deciding which flag, standard, banner or drape was carried by each respective service or organisation. It is even less surprising when one considers the many thousands of patterns of flags and banners extant during those short, but turbulent, 13 years of the 'Thousand Year Reich'.

In this small volume, we have provided a general but concise guide to the more important and frequently encountered Colours.

We must emphasise, however, that this book contains a selection of the many flags used and gives only the more important items; it would need another volume the size of this one to cover them all. Where known the dimensions of these are given. Where we have been unable to trace specific details we have estimated the sizes purely as a guide.

In compiling this work the authors are greatly indebted to the many individuals who have provided material both from their own collections and files, and without whose generous assistance the scope of this work would have been greatly restricted. In particular our special thanks go to: Bob Anderson; Ed Anderson; Eric Campion; Marc and Lee-Ann Brown; Philip Capewell; Dr K.-G. Klietmann; Walt Nichols; Rolfe Holbrook; Joe Pankowski; Robert Strodel; Andrew Mollo, Historical Research Unit; Laurence Milner, Imperial War Museum; Messrs Wallis and Wallis; Roy Smith; Peter Seymour; Edward Kenton; Richard E. Deeter; all of whom gave major advice and contributions.

Special thanks to Charles Scaglione and Major John R. Angolia for their considerable efforts in locating many of the fine Standards shown within and, finally, to Frederick J. Stephens, who not only suggested the basic concept, but whose valuable guidance has seen the book through to completion.

All photographic illustrations are from the collections of the authors, except where otherwise stated.

Andrew S. Walker
Ron G. Hickox
Chris Farlowe
July, 1973

ABOVE: A gigantic version of the Führer Standard (see also page 33) hanging above the entrance of the Congress Hall at the Luitpoldhain, part of the Nürnberg Rally Grounds. The flags on either side are the standard State or National colours.

CONTENTS

Note: Only the fifth and eleventh colour plates in this book fall in sequence in their respective sections; the remainder are placed on individual pages and are cross referenced to their relevant sections and pages therein.

Flags in the Third Reich

DURING the week-long Party Rallies in Nürnberg each September from 1933 to 1938, the processional route of the march past through the streets of the old mediaeval city was festively decorated with swastika banners and flags of all types. As well as the house flags the photograph below shows a specially designed decorative banner featuring the National Emblem. The purpose of these banners does not indicate membership of any organisation, but is merely an expression of sympathy to the cause they represent.

The public display of the swastika was not confined to within the borders of Nazi Germany during the 1930s, and sympathisers and affiliated organisations abroad existed almost undisturbed, not only in the USA but also in Great Britain. Shown here are members of the German Veterans Association in November, 1936, laying a wreath at the spot where a German Zeppelin was shot down over England in 1916. The German delegation is supported by members of the 'Britisch Legion' of Great Burstead, flying the Union Jack alongside the emblem that would one day enslave Europe.

All or most of the banners carried by the many organisations of the Third Reich were made by master craftsmen with the embroidery and intricate detail applied by hand at each stage of manufacture. Smaller pennants and the like were machined. The photographic sequence on this and the following three pages shows the progress of several different types of flag from the initial designs to completion, taken from an issue of *Die Wehrmacht,* a German military magazine of the Third Reich era.

ABOVE: The designer and painter, Paul Casberg, who was responsible for the creation of many accoutrements—including the design of the German Army dagger—at work in his studio on an Army Truppenfahne.

LEFT: Continuing the old tradition of a single facings banner, separately embroidered on each side, the first stage in the manufacture of a Standard comprised the tracing of the basic design on to a silk base.

LEFT: The silk base was stretched on a special frame and carefully embroidered by skilled workers, one woman to each side. As the sections of the design were finished the flag was wound up on to the upper roller so that the surface was taut at all times, thus ensuring there were no distortions in patterning.

RIGHT: Final details and basic designs were finished on the vertical frame before transfer to a horizontal frame for highlighting of the smaller symbols.

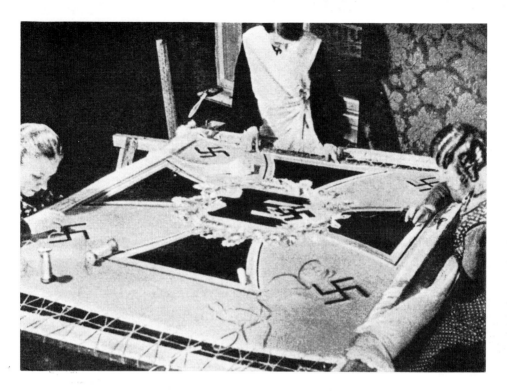

ABOVE: The edgings of the banner completed on the horizontal frame; note the silver cotton on the left used to highlight the edging of the swastika.

BELOW: The finalised banner, 120cm square, secured with special brass tacks to its pole.

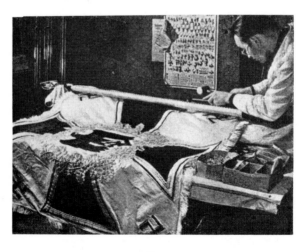

ABOVE: NSDAP Organisational banners being machined. The banner in the foreground is a half-completed NSKK Company Pennant, and that in the centre an NSBO District Banner. BELOW: Silk screen printed flags of various patterns drying in a controlled-temperature room to prevent uneven colour distribution.

OPPOSITE, TOP: An official store room of completed, but unissued, flags, banners and poles.

BELOW: March past in the 1920s by members of the Freikoros and right-wing associations. The flags display a combination of both the Prussian War Flag of the 1867 North German Confederation, together with the 'Death or Glory' skull-and-crossbones-inspired variations of the new National Socialists' flag. Both designs were in the black, white and red National Colours.

NSDAP

Hoheitsfahne (Area Banner) of the Kreisleitung or Area Leadership of München. Banner is of woollen material dyed scarlet with silver fringe. Central device is a black mobile swastika on a white circle. Administrative patch is of red-brown velvet with white Gothic lettering.

Dimensions:
140cm x 120cm;
patch 21cm x 16cm
with 1cm white border
circle diameter 90cm;
swastika 60cm x 12cm

THE Political Leaders of the Nationalsozialistische Deutsche Arbeiterpartei German National Socialists' Party were in charge of the indoctrination, planning and government of the German people in each of the 920 areas of responsibility designated by the Führer. Like all other Nazi Party organisations each level had its own flag or banner to identify it at Party meetings. Districts were indicated by a small name patch in the upper left canton. Affiliated associations such as the German Labour Front, the Factory Cell Organisation, the SS, SA, Hitler Youth, etc, had a similar system of identification for their banners, while the Factory Cell Organisations bore black patches featuring the

Ortsgruppenfahne (Local Group Banner) of the Ortsgruppenleiter or Local Group Leader of Altdorf. Banner is of woollen material dyed scarlet with silver fringe. Central device is a black mobile swastika on a white circle. Administrative patch is of light brown cloth with white Gothic lettering.

Dimensions:
140cm x 120cm;
patch 21cm x 16cm
with 1cm light brown
cloth border;
circle diameter 90cm;
swastika 60cm x 12cm

ABOVE: A Parade of Party Banners, Tempelhofer Feld in Berlin, May Day, 1935

name of the Factory together with its District. In all cases for these organisations the size of the flag was 140cm x 120cm, usually edged with a silver fringe. The flag was fastened to a two-section pole by seven nickel-plated rings, the top of the pole bearing a metal device, usually the symbol of each respective organisation.

A unique banner was the Standard of the Schlageter Memorial Association, of the Hannover District. Albert Leo Schlageter was given the status of martyr by the National Socialists following his execution by a French firing squad in 1923, for the sabotaging of a Radio Station in the Ruhr district occupied by the French following the Treaty of Versailles. Schlageter had been one of a number of right-wing extremists dedicated to the expulsion of the Occupation Authorities from German soil. This actual banner, the only one of its kind, has surprisingly enough survived the war.

The ground of the banner is white on both sides, with the obverse featuring a hand-embroidered central device in black, and the Imperial Battle Flag

embroidered in the top left-hand corner in red, black and white. The date '1923', and the legend below the swastika, is printed in black. The reverse has an embroidered Prussian Eagle in black, gold and grey. The banner is edged on the four sides with heavy black cord.

In 1935 the Schlageter Memorial Association was disbanded, and the banner stored in a private museum in the Hannover District.

Dimensions: 180cm square (approx.)
Eric Campion collection

A large stone memorial bearing a huge cross was erected to the memory of Schlageter near Düsseldorff. Inaugurated on the tenth anniversary of Schlageter's death, June 4, 1933, this photograph shows the banner being carried in the presence of State and Party dignitaries. Note the unusual manner of suspension on the pole.

ABOVE: Gorget for Political Leader Standard Bearers, bronze finished, introduced circa 1938.

BELOW: Car pennant for Kreisleiter (District Leader). It has silver devices on gold and white with red edging. **Dimensions: 35cm square**

LEFT: Factory Cell (NSBO) Standard pole top, nickel-plate finish over brass, with black background to swastika on hammer head.

BELOW: First pattern Standard pole top for Political Leader Banners, nickel-plated with black painted swastika.

ABOVE: Second pattern Standard pole top for Political Leader banners in the style of the redesigned National Emblem (*Hoheitsalszeichen*) of 1936. In cast and polished aluminium, the swastika is again painted black.

LEFT: Hoheitsfahne of an NSBO Factory of District 3. Colours as for Political Leader's banner.

RIGHT: Hoheitsfahne of the German Labour Front (DAF). Colour details as for Political Leader's banner but with black edged white area patch, and black cogwheel symbol trimmed with white.

Dimensions: 140cm x 120cm; patch 21cm x 16cm with 1cm white edging; cogwheel diameter 70cm; circle diameter 60cm

BELOW: Standard Bearers of the NSBO marching through the streets of Nürnberg, at the Reichsparteitag, September, 1933. Note the different patterns of pole top.

An unusual example of a War Merit version of the banner of the German Labour Front. The edging to the cogwheel and swastika is in silver braid, and the distinctive feature of an embroidered silver bullion War Service Cross is placed in the top right canton—a decoration possibly intended as an award to the company for outstanding war production. This banner is additionally unusual in that it features no identification patch in the upper left canton. The ground of the banner is red silk and not the more commonly encountered flag cloth.

Fanfare trumpeter of the German Labour Front (DAF). Banner is red with silver fringe, black cogwheel and swastika on a white ground, and is double-sided.

BELOW: Rudolf Hess, Hitler's Secretary and Deputy Führer, congratulating workers at the Krupp Armaments Factory, May 11, 1940. The standards shown are Musterbetriebsfahnen (Banners of the élite corps of the German Labour Front), and are distinguished by having a gold fringe and cogwheel outlined in black. These were awarded to units within the factory who had given outstanding services to the Party and State.

Dimensions: As for Hoheitsfahne

Musterbetriebsfahnen of the German Labour Front in the Congress Hall at a Nürnberg Party Rally, 1937.

Dimensions: As for Hoheitsfahne

ABOVE: Prior to the establishment of the National Agricultural Association (Reichsnähstand) this photograph shows the very first flag awarded under the National Socialist Government to German Agricultural workers (Bauernschaften), on December 3, 1933, in the village of Gross-Laash in Mecklenburg. The flag is black, and bears a silver plough surmounted by a red sword.

LEFT: The reverse of a Standard pole top of the Reichsnährstand, displaying a gilded sword and ear-of-corn devices on a polished nickel swastika.

The opening of the Agricultural Exhibition in the Hamburg Bauerliches Brauchtum, June, 1935. A parade of mounted agricultural workers starts the proceedings with a display of Association Standards. Colouring was red with silver edging and had gold or silver devices embroidered thereon.

BELOW : Massed banners of the Physical Training League at a sports meeting, 1937. The flag ground is red, and bears a black sports-pattern eagle with swastika on a vertical white panel with circular section. In the upper canton of each flag can be seen the black, silver-edged patch, upon which in silver bullion lettering appear details of the district and activities. (See also page 27.)

ABOVE: Fanfare trumpeters of the Physical Training League. The banner was red on white with black eagle and silver fringing.

RIGHT: A Standard of the Physical Training League being presented by the National Sports Leader, von Tschammer und Osten. The standard was red and white with black eagle and gold oak leaf surround.

A banner of the Physical Training League, District 11, Shooting Association of St Johannes von Nep, Havert. Banner is red with white centre and swastika, black eagle and identification patch.

RAD

THE National Labour Service (Reichsarbeitsdienst—RAD) was compulsory
enlistment for all German males prior to service in the armed forces. Its fore-
runner, the FAD or Voluntary Labour Service (Freiwilliges Arbeitsdienst),
although formed earlier, was not properly uniformed until early 1933. Its

insignia was composed of stylised wheatsheaves with a square-tipped spade, which was altered during 1934 to a trowel-ended spade.

OPPOSITE PAGE: Fanfare trumpeter of the RAD Reichschule (RS). (See also page 39.) The unit title, in abbreviated form, is embroidered on the banner.

ABOVE: An FAD unit in May 1933 with the first pattern banner which bears no swastika or unit identification. The ground is red, with the black emblem on a white shield and silver fringing.

BELOW: The 1934 pattern Abteilungsfahne of the RAD (the Abteilung was the local district command, approximately equivalent to the Orstgruppe or local area of the Political Leadership). The banner is double sided and bears the embroidered RAD device in black and white, over a large white edged black swastika, on a red field. Identification of the unit is embroidered in the upper fly. This banner is carried by members of a Bezirkschule—District School.

ABOVE: Fanfare trumpeters of the RAD in 1934; note the banners bear the earlier FAD devices, and the new swastika of the State. Ground is red and white with black devices fringed in white.

Dimensions: 45cm x 40cm

BELOW: General Service Flag of RAD Camps and Establishments. Red and white ground with black device.

Dimensions: 90cm x 60cm

OPPOSITE PAGE: Constantin Hierl, Commander of the RAD, showing his personal Command Standard. Red, white and black ground with black device.

ABOVE: A detachment of RAD Standard Bearers on parade in Nürnberg, 1937. Note the Standard Bearer's gorget in wear. (See also page 38.)

LEFT: RAD Abteilungsfahne. Ground is red and white with silver fringing and black and white embroidered devices. Administrative patch in red is carried in the upper right canton.

**Dimensions:
135cm square**

32

ABOVE: The Führer Standard

Dimensions: 135cm square

BELOW LEFT: Vehicle Pennant of the Leader of the State Labour Service (DAF).

BELOW RIGHT: An original double-sided and finely embroidered silk banner of the NSDAP Old Guard (Alte Garde)—those who took part in the November 9, 1923, putsch. The function of this banner is unknown.

Dimensions: 45cm square
Major John R. Angolia collection

ABOVE: An RAD Standard Bearer at a public meeting in Vienna, after the annexation of Austria, 1938. Clearly visible is the aluminium Standard pole top, bearing spade and wheatsheaves device, the gorget and the bandolier. (See also page 38.) The latter is brown with two broad braid bands in silver wire, into which are woven a repeating design of RAD emblems.

OPPOSITE PAGE: Two detail photographs of an Abteilungsfahne. The upper photograph shows the embroidered patch bearing the name of the unit 'Ernst Albrecht von Eberstein'. The heavily embroidered central emblem can be seen in the lower photograph.

RIGHT: The SA Regimental Standard with the motto Deutschland Erwache: Germany Awake. The SS Regimental Standard was identical to the SA pattern with the exception of the black background to the nameplate.

**Dimensions:
60cm x 70cm**

BELOW: Silk Company Flag of the SA, 1st Company Bodyguard (Leib) Regiment, Group Hochland.

**Dimensions:
130cm x 140cm**

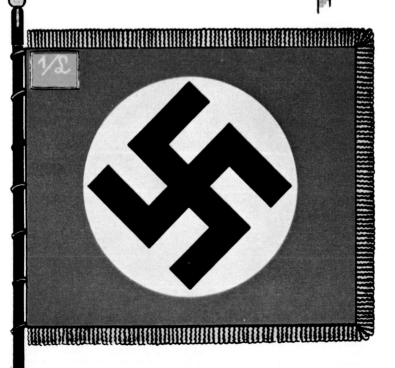

Political Leaders' Vehicle Pennants flown on the right side at the front.

**Dimensions: 29cm square and
40cm x 25cm pointed**

Reichsleiter   Reichsleitung Departmental Heads

Gauleiter   Gauleitung Departmental Heads
                                and Deputy Gauleiter

Kreisleiter   Kreisleitung Departmental Heads

ABOVE: Gorget for Standard Bearer of the RAD. Polished nickel plate finish with the motto of the Labour Service 'Arbeit Adelt'—Labour ennobles—engraved on to the shield. The central emblem, a separate fixture, is of a dull finish.

Dimensions: 16cm x 20cm

Bob Anderson collection

OPPOSITE PAGE, TOP:

Photograph taken during the Labour Service Ceremonies at a Nürnberg Rally show trumpet banners bearing the identification marks of the Reichsschule (State School) establishment.

OPPOSITE PAGE, BOTTOM:

The basic trumpet banner. (See also page 41.)

NSKK Command Post Flags

Commander-in-Chief

High Command

Training Inspectorate

National School for Leaders

Motor-Obergruppe

Motor-Gruppe (Division)

Motor-Brigade

Motor-Standarte (Regiment)

Mottor-Staffel (Battalion)

Motor Vehicle and Motor Cycle Pennant

Dimensions: 35cm square; 35cm square; 30cm square; 30cm square; 30cm square; 30cm square; 35cm x 25cm; 20cm square; 20cm x 30cm pointed

ABOVE: A fine example of a heavily embroidered silk Labour Service (RAD) trumpet banner, bearing the Abteilung number 294.

Dimensions: 45cm x 40cm

Charles Scaglione collection

41

ABOVE: From 1941, Honour Ribbons were awarded to certain units of the Reichs Arbeitsdienst in recognition of special services performed since 1938. The ribbon was suspended from the unit's banner and was dark brown with a black and white strip along each side. A special clasp was fastened to the ribbon which bore the year of the award and the name of the area or province in which the unit had served with distinction. Further and later distinctions were indicated by bars which were attached to the ribbon beneath the clasp. The photographs above show in actual size one of these clasps, which although dated 1940 bears no name in the central panel, thus indicating that it is an unissued piece. The badge is silver coloured (plated) and bears the Assmann trademark on the reverse.

Polizei

Following the rise to power of Hitler, units of the Weimarian Police adopted the emblems of National Socialism. The above photo shows members of the Berlin Police on Labour Day (May 1st) 1933 carrying the newly adopted swastika banner.

ABOVE: Unit Pennant of a BDM Mädelgruppe.

Dimensions: 70cm pointed, approx.

Major John R. Angolia collection

BELOW: Obverse of Deutsche Jungvolk Unit Pennant with an honorary title and emblem, 'Andreas-Hofer'.

Dimensions: 60cm pointed, approx.

Major John R. Angolia collection

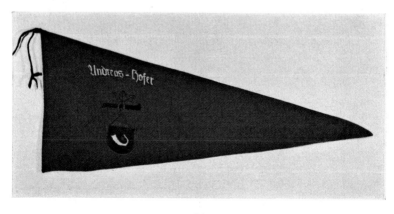

Hitler Youth Car Pennants flown on the right side at the front.

Dimensions: 30cm square, approx.

Staff Leader of the RJF.

Departmental Heads of the RJF.

HJ District Leaders.

BELOW: Legion Condor Standard. The banner displays a silver bullion Luftwaffe eagle and swastika superimposing an Iron Cross, on a scarlet silk ground, quartered by a yellow gold cross which bears in the corners the Luftwaffe eagle and swastika, the Condor Eagle, the initials LC, and the Falange of Arrows breaking the Moorish Yoke. Note also the fine bullion gold and red bandolier worn by the Standard Bearer.

ABOVE: Detail of an early Police unit banner, the unit patch in black and edged in silver cord, embroidered with the Police emblem in white and black. From about 1937 the patch featured the eagle and wreath Police emblem, embroidered in white on a green ground.

On the 1st April 1933, the Prussian Schutzpolizer were awarded their own colours, which included an unusual Standard (shown below). Loosely based on the design of the SA/SS Regimental Standard, the banner features the Prussian Police Star in each of its four corners.

ABOVE: Obverse and Reverse of Luftwaffe Signals Unit Standard.

Dimensions: 140cm square, approx.

Charles Scaglione collection

BELOW AND OPPOSITE PAGE: Obverse and Reverse of a silk Luftwaffe Trumpet Banner for the flying school at Stendal.

Dimensions: 60cm x 40cm, approx.

Charles Scaglione collection

ABOVE: 1935 version Command flag of the Reichsminister of Aviation and Supreme Commander of the Airforce (Herman Göring). A later pattern is identical but features in addition crossed Field Marshal's Batons between the swastika and the Pour le Merite.

ABOVE: Prussian Police fanfare trumpeters at the Olympic Games, Berlin, 1936. Banners are green and silver with black device.

OPPOSITE PAGE: Formations of the Police at Nürnberg, 1937, having just received their new-styled colours, and wearing the newly introduced Police gorget and bandolier.

ABOVE: Police Trumpet Banner, late pattern, silver embroidered on green silk.

Dimensions: 40cm square, approx.

Charles Scaglione collection

BELOW: Standard of the Reichsministers der Luftfahrt (Commander of the Air Service). Also C-in-C Luftwaffe.

ABOVE: Standard of the Commander in Chief of the Armed Forces, 1935 pattern. Printed on red woollen flag material.

LEFT: Standard of the Commander in Chief of the Navy.

Stahlhelm

THE Stahlhelm, a soldiers' veterans' association, flourished during the 1920s and 1930s, but was absorbed into the SS and SA during 1933 and 1934.

ABOVE: Franz Seldte (left), leader of the Stahlhelm. His personal standard is carried on his right. Note the gorgets worn by the standard bearers.

LEFT: Personal standard of the Stahlhelm-Bundesführer, Franz Seldte. The design features the Prussian eagle and Imperial crown.

OPPOSITE: Three Stahlhelm standard bearers at a parade in 1933.

ABOVE LEFT: Naval Standard, blue silk.

Dimensions: 125cm x 125cm

ABOVE RIGHT: Luftwaffe Standard, red silk, Flak Artillery.

Dimensions: 125cm x 125cm

BELOW LEFT: Army Cavalry Regimental Standard. Orange silk.

BELOW RIGHT: Army Company Flag, Pioneer. Black silk.

Dimensions: 125cm x 125cm

These illustrations are from a series of original postcards identifying military banner patterns.

Major John R. Angolia collection

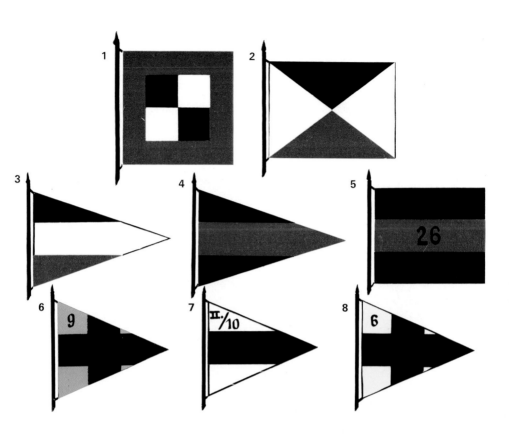

ABOVE: **Command and Staff Flags of the Army.**
1. Army Group, 2. Army Corps, 3. Army Division, 4. Artillery Staff Command, 5. Artillery Regimental Staff, 6. Transport Unit Staff, 7. Infantry Battalion Staff, 8. Signals Section Staff.

RIGHT: Armoured Unit Regimental Standard. Pink silk.

Dimensions not known

Gorget for standard and banner bearers of the Stahlhelm. Silver coloured, cast in one piece.

Dimensions: 14cm x 18cm

ABOVE: Obverse and reverse of a finely embroidered Stahlhelm trumpet banner. The silver steel helmet is superimposed over black, white and red. The fringing is gold-coloured medal bullion. Note the similarity of the design to the reverse of the Bundesführer Standard shown on page 54.

BELOW, LEFT: Bundesgründer-Fahne. RIGHT: Bundesfahne.

Command Flags, Car Pennants and Table Drape of the NSKOV, the National Socialist Organisation for the Relief of War Victims.

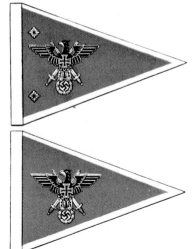

TOP AND CENTRE: Stahlhelm banners, displaying emblems.

BOTTOM: Youth-Stahlhelm banners.

Allgemeine and Waffen-SS

AFTER the defeat of Germany the Russians captured numerous standards from the Zeughaus in Berlin.

OPPOSITE PAGE: During the victory celebrations in Moscow the standard of Waffen-SS Division Leibstandarte Adolf Hitler was paraded as a victory trophy before the Lenin Mausoleum. Here it is seen minus the banner. BELOW: Close-up of the Standard head with a small crudely applied Reichskriegsflagge with tasselling added to simulate the correct banner which should be hung there.

ABOVE: The regimental band of the 67th Allgemeine-SS Regiment parading through the town of Heiligenstadt in August, 1935. Although strictly not a Standard, the Schellenbaum, or 'Jingling Johnny', seen in this photograph, bears near the top a small silver and black embroidered drape on which is the device of the Death's Head. This drape, in various forms for different organisa-

tions, is one of the essential features of the Schellenbaum, as both a decorative aid and means of identification. The colours of these drapes, which are usually heavily fringed and tasselled, conform to the Service Organisation. For example, those carried by Luftwaffe bands were usually grey/blue; by SA and Political Leaders bright red; and so on.

ABOVE: Sturmbannführer Jacob Grimminger, the Colour Bearer of the 'Blood Flag', at the head of an SS detachment at a Nürnberg Party Rally leading a parade through the streets of Nürnberg. The 'Blood Flag' (Blutfahne) was so called as this was the actual banner carried at the head of the Nazi detachment when they were fired upon by the Police during the Munich 'putsch' of November 9, 1923. The flag was splattered with the blood of those shot during this encounter, and was thereafter considered to be a 'Holy Relic'.

OPPOSITE PAGE: Regimental Standards of the SS awaiting consecration by Hitler in the Luitpoldhain Stadium at Nürnberg. The Standard Bearers are wearing the first pattern SA/SS gorgets, together with the early narrow leather bandolier. The nameplates of the SS Standards are of black background with silver script whilst those of the SA are red with silver script (see page 36). RIGHT: Massed standards of the SS Regiments. Note the reverse of the banners are identical to those of the SA, bearing below the swastika the legend 'Sturmabteilung' (Storm Troops) and not 'Schutzstaffel'.

BELOW: A line-up of SA and SS Standards outside the Congress Hall, Nürnberg, September, 1938. Grimminger and the Blutfahne to the fore of the assembled Standard Bearers.

Standards of SS Regiments, clearly showing the head of the standard pole and banner design, at one of the Nürnberg rallies.

Dimensions of banner: 60cm x 70cm

ABOVE: At the 1938 Party Rally in Nürnberg Hitler presents to the SS Officer
an SS Sturmbannfahne (Battalion Flag).
   Shown very clearly in this photograph is the gorget introduced in the same
year for SS Standard Bearers. Also worn is the bandolier, a detailed photograph
of which appears on page 82.
   Original photograph by Photo-Hilz, Nürnberg A, Theatergasse 13, in the
collection of the author.

ABOVE: In the Congress Hall at Nürnberg, the Standard bearer of the regiment 'LAH' (on right of photo) can be seen wearing the special 'LAH' gorget, which differed considerably from the usual pattern. The exact design of this gorget is not known (at the time of publication) although it is possible that the central emblem between the pairs of crossed Standards consists, in part, of the inter-twined 'LAH' device. The corner studs appear to bear the SS runes.

OPPOSITE PAGE, TOP: An actual, original example of the SS second pattern gorget in dull nickel finish with black oxidised silver eagle and swastika.

Dimensions: 20cm broad

OPPOSITE PAGE, BOTTOM: The SA, NSKK and also first pattern SS, gorget. Polished silvered shield bearing gilt finish corner bosses and sunburst, and silvered central emblem.

Dimensions: 12cm broad

ABOVE: The Regimental Standard of the SS 'Leibstandarte Adolf Hitler' on parade beneath one of the gigantic bronze eagles in the Luitpold field at the Nürnberg rally grounds. The photograph shows the Standard with the 'Deutschland Erwache' banner. Also visible is the special gorget worn by the bearer of this particular Standard. A more detailed photograph showing this gorget appears on page 71.

BELOW: The Regimental Standard of the LAH was, some time after the outbreak of World War 2, considerably altered insofar as a completely new banner was designed. This banner, although very similar to Hitler's personal Standard (see page 33), bears four 'open-winged' National emblems. A gold coloured fringe and tassels hang from three sides of the banner. The photograph shows, on the left, Heinrich Himmler, Reichsführer-SS, and on the right, SS-Obergruppenführer Sepp Dietrich, Commander of the LAH, with the new banner, at the presentation of the new Standard.

ABOVE: The new Führer pattern Standard of the LAH at the head of a parade in Metz during 1944.

BELOW: SS Cavalry Regiments carried a distinctive Standard quite unlike that of regular foot regiments. This rare photograph shows the Standard of the Seventh SS-Reiterabschnitt at a parade in the Berlin Lustgarten. The distinctive feature of this Standard is the black patch bearing a crossed lance device, together with the unit designation.

ABOVE: Obverse and reverse views of an SS Regimental trumpet banner, in this case of the Fourth SS Deathshead (Totenkopf) Regiment. Fine quality silver embroidery on a black background.

Dimensions: 50cm x 40cm approx.

ABOVE: Each SS Battalion carried its own Colour, known as the Sturmbann-fahne. The brilliant red flag carries a large black swastika on a white circular field on both sides. In the upper canton alongside the black lacquered two-section pole is a black patch embroidered in silver thread with the Battalion and Regimental number. The patch is edged with a silver wire cord, and appears on both sides of the flag. The flag is edged in a black and silver fringe. (*Close-up details of this pattern are shown at left and on page 79.*) Of interest is the fact that the photograph reproduced above features the 'static' swastika. The static swastika appears to have given way to a 'mobile' swastika (angled on point) on most NSDP organisational banners after about 1933. However, for traditional reasons, some units continued to carry the early pattern on occasions, contrary to general regulations.

Dimensions: 140cm x 130cm

OPPOSITE PAGE, TOP: Massed Battalion Colours of the SS at the Nürnberg Rally, 1933. Note the third flag from the left, bearing the patch of an SS-Verfugungstruppe Unit. OPPOSITE PAGE, BOTTOM: SS Cavalry Standards at a parade in Berlin, November, 1935. Note the gorgets in wear. ABOVE: A detail section of an SS Battalion Flag, showing approximately half actual size the silver threaded black fringe, and the unit patch. The Battalion number is always embroidered in Roman numerals, whilst that of the Regiment is always featured in Arabic numerals.

ABOVE: The Battalion Flag of the Fifth Battalion SS Regiment 'Totenkopf' paraded in Austria, 1938. Note the broad bandolier worn by the Standard Bearer. This is illustrated in detail on page 82.

BELOW: Gauleiter Albert Forster, at right, presenting the Banner of the SS-Heimwehr Danzig, August, 1939. The flag features a Deathshead super-imposing a swastika, on a white field, with red background quartered by black cross-stripes displaying the SS runes and the Crown and Crosses of the Free State of Danzig.

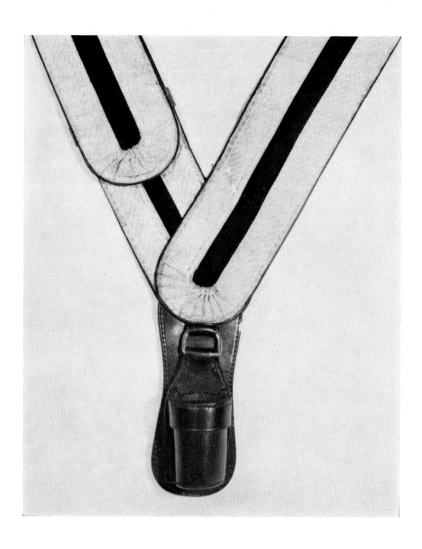

ABOVE: A view of the lower section of the bandolier worn by SS Standard Bearers. The 'bucket' in which the pole base sits is black leather, the bandolier *per se* is black leather decorated with heavy silver-coloured braid.

Andrew Mollo collection

BELOW: One of the more outstanding features of military bands were the highly ornate kettle drum covers. This illustration shows a kettle drummer of the band of the SS-Leibstandarte Adolf Hitler, July, 1935. The covers were of black silk with silver devices and fringing.

BELOW: SS Command Flags and Vehicle Pennants made of waterproof cloth in black and white with rustproof thread and covered in a transparent cellophane cover in inclement weather.

Reichsführer-SS

**Dimensions: 60cm square
with 1cm silver border**

Central Department
Head

Dimensions: 70cm x 40cm

Departmental Head

Dimensions: 70cm x 40cm

SS District

Dimensions: 70cm x 40cm

SS Sub-District

Dimensions: 70cm x 40cm

SS Regiment

Dimensions: 50cm x 2

SS Battalion

**Dimensions:
22cm x 33cm**

SS Vehicle Pennant

**Dimensions:
25cm x 40cm**

SS Vehicle Pennant for
Fordende Mitglieder or
Supporting Member.

Dimensions: 22cm x 35cm

ABOVE: An SS Vehicle Pennant, shown out of its case, and also contained in its original celluloid leatherbound weatherproof case. Dimensions given on opposite page.

Roy Smith collection

ABOVE: An original SS District Command Flag, double sided, in black and white silk with silver embroidered eagle. The District name 'Rhein' is embroidered in silver thread in outline form only.   *Andrew Mollo collection*

OPPOSITE PAGE, TOP: Norwegian recruits of the Waffen-SS taking the Oath of Loyalty, showing the Standard of the 'Wiking' Battalion, October, 1941.

OPPOSITE PAGE, BOTTOM: Flemish SS Volunteer Unit with their Standard, September, 1941.

BELOW: Members of the Dutch SS displaying their highly unusual banners. Colour details and dimensions uncertain. Probably black, yellow and red.

BELOW: Standard of the Danish Waffen-SS Foreign Volunteer Unit, white cross on red woollen cloth.

Dimensions: 130cm x 100cm approx.

OPPOSITE PAGE: Newly awarded National Socialist Motor Corps (NSKK) Company pennants being consecrated against an SA Standard.

NSKK

OPPOSITE PAGE: Hitler awarding NSKK Regiments with new Standards, Nürnberg. Note the cloth patch bearing the unit designation at the top of the Standard. Red on white silk with black/white/red edging and black administrative patch in upper left canton.

Dimensions: 70cm x 70cm approx.

ABOVE: Kettle Drummer of the Motorised 'Cavalry' (NSKK). Black with silver devices.

BELOW LEFT: The aluminium Car Pennant pole top of the NSKK (the reverse is identical). Similar tops of the emblems of other organisations are frequently encountered. BELOW RIGHT: The NSKK Motor Wheel emblem. This patch appears on both sides of the Company Pennant and on the reverse side only of the Regimental Standard.

ABOVE: Fanfare trumpeters of the 58th Regiment. Banners are black with white or silver devices and fringing.

OPPOSITE PAGE: NSKK Korpsführer Hühnlein in conversation with the Standard Bearer of the 78th Regiment. Although not shown here, until about 1935 NSKK Standard Bearers wore the SA/SS gorget (see page 70). Thereafter a new pattern was introduced, together with a bandolier, that bore the NSKK version of the National emblem.

SA

The SA or Sturmabteilung were the 'private army' of the Nazi Party and were originally formed to provide protection from opponents at Party meetings and to assume a propaganda function by way of marches and parades. BELOW: SA Regimental Standard Bearers outside the Congress Hall in Nürnberg, wearing the newly introduced bandoliers, which were similar to the SS bandolier shown on page 83, but with silver braid on a coloured background. OPPOSITE PAGE: A further view of the Blutfahne during the award of new SA Regimental Standards at Nürnberg. The standards were 'consecrated' by being touched with the Blood Flag by Hitler.

Hitler Youth— HJ, DJ and BDM

ABOVE: An original example of a Deutsche Jungvolk Jungbannfahne. The emblem and scroll are worked on the black cotton field in a heavy woven silk material. The pole top, of which a detail appears opposite, is cast aluminium.

Dimensions: 160cm x 120cm

LEFT: The cast aluminium pole top used for DJ banners. Inscribed in the metal is the DJ eagle and the NSDAP diamond and swastika badge. The same design appears on the reverse, the eagle's head turned the other way.

Dimension: 30cm high

BELOW: Jacob Grimminger, bearer of the 'Blutfahne', in conversation with a Hitler Youth Standard Bearer. Note the sleeve insignia which comprises a silver coloured eagle on a blue-black ground, bearing the red/white/black HJ diamond insignia.

ABOVE: A DJ trumpet banner, featuring the single white rune on a black ground. The edge of the banner features a white cotton fringing.

Dimensions: 40cm x 40cm

BELOW: A DJ *Jungenschaft* pennant of red cotton with white taping, bearing the commemorative name of the unit 'Blücher' after the famous Prussian Field Marshal. Obverse is black with a single white name.

Eric Campion collection
Dimensions: 30cm x 60cm

ABOVE: Fanfare Trumpeters of the DJ at the Nürnberg Rally in 1937. A detail view of this banner is shown on the opposite page.

ABOVE: Deutsche Jungvolk fanfare trumpeter, 1934. The trumpet banner has
the unusual triangular curved arm 'sunwheel' swastika. Black cloth with white
device.

Dimensions: 36cm x 50cm

ABOVE: A gathering of DJ trumpeters with the rarely seen DJ trumpet banner flighted eagle device, 1941. Ground is black with white devices and fringing. The scroll panel above the eagle contains the Bann or District number.

BELOW: Landjahr Hitler Youth, or HJ personnel serving in agricultural and other land duties had a special trumpet banner of white cloth with black gothic lettering and white fringing.

ABOVE: Hitler Youth Standard Bearers with early type Gefolgschaft banners at the Nürnberg Parteitag, September, 1933. Heading the march is the banner bearing the commemorative title of the Nazi martyr 'Horst Wessel'. The banners feature a coloured patch in the upper left corner on which is embroidered the unit designation. Ground was red and white with black device and patch.

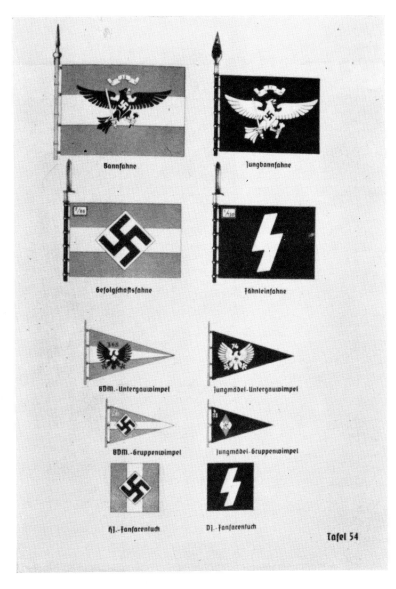

Bannfahne

Jungbannfahne

Gefolgschaftsfahne

Fähnleinfahne

BDM.-Untergauwimpel

Jungmädel-Untergauwimpel

BDM.-Gruppenwimpel

Jungmädel-Gruppenwimpel

HJ.-Fanfarentuch

DJ.-Fanfarentuch

Tafel 54

HJ and DJ banners, 1943

LEFT TO RIGHT, TOP TO BOTTOM : The Bann Flag, red, black and white with the Bann number displayed in the scroll at the top ; DJ Bann flag, black and white with the Jungbann number shown in the scroll. Gefolgschaft banner, styled like the HJ armband, with the Unterbann and Gefolgschaft's number shown in the patch on the top left corner ; Jungbann banner, all black with white seig rune, and showing the Stamm and Fahnlein numbers. BDM and JM platoon pennants. HJ and DJ bugle banners.

RIGHT: The Hitler Youth Standard Bearer's gorget. This was made in white metal and was carried under the collar by chain links.

BELOW: An unusual and distinctive early banner, circa 1934, of a unit of the Hitler Youth flight training section. The colours of the Fliegerjugend banner shown are uncertain but the background is believed to be sky blue, the glider red and white, and the legend panel (upper canton) black with white or silver lettering. This identifies the unit.

Hitler Youth Fanfare Trumpeter in the Berlin Lustgarten, May 1, 1935. This banner is unusual in that the white field runs horizontally and not vertically, and that the unit's number is embroidered at the top.

Gefolgschaft

Hauptmann Berthold

ABOVE: An interesting display of early DJ Fahleinfahne, some featuring the honoured names of the units. Circa 1934.

BELOW: A DJ *Jungenschafts* pennant, white on black. *Eric Campion collection*

Dimensions: 50cm x 75cm

OPPOSITE PAGE: The obverse and reverse of an original trumpet banner of a unit which was permitted to bear the name of Captain Berthold, a distinguished German flying ace. The fringing is gold coloured (as opposed to the normal white cotton), the field on the reverse side is black, bearing a red sunrise, yellow propeller and white inscription.

ABOVE: Reichsjugendfuhrer Artur Axman presenting HJ Standards, Prague, November 1940.

Heer (Army)

The Reichskriegflagge (war flag) was the national flag used by the Army and Air Force. In the national colours of red, white, and black, it included the old traditional cross in the upper canton and the swastika as the central device. Sizes range from small pennant size types through to large patterns over 900cm in length.

Until 1936 the German Army continued to carry their traditional Imperial Standards. In that year, however, Hitler ordered the creation of new Standards (see pages 10–12), the first presentations taking place at the Nürnberg Rally in the September of that year. Two patterns were designed, the large one being 120cm sq. (the *Truppenfahne*) for battalions. Regiments had the smaller 'Swallow tail' Regimental Standard of which examples are shown in the colour plates.

BELOW: Swearing the Oath of Loyalty on a Regimental Standard. Of note is the decorative pike head and the standard bearer's gorget plate and bandolier.

Traditional Imperial Standards paraded at a memorial service for the German dead of the Great War, Tannenberg August 27, 1933. President Hindenburg takes the salute. This was before the adoption of the new Nazi regime standards which kept to the size and general style of the old standards but incorporated swastika devices in the design.

FOLLOWING PAGE, ABOVE : Swearing the Oath of Loyalty on a Battalion flag. Battalion flags were presented only to Infantry (White) ; Jäger (Green) ; and Engineer (Black) units.

FOLLOWING PAGE, BELOW : The Army Standard Bearer's gorget, a matt silver finished shield with the central emblem, and the oak leaves in each corner, in an oxydised finish. The chains bear alternately the National emblem and an oak leaf cluster. It is shown in wear on the previous page.

PREVIOUS PAGE, TOP: Army trumpeters in 1933, wearing the old Reichsheer pattern uniforms, present a fanfare displaying the highly ornate Imperial trumpet banners and kettle drum drapes. BELOW: A section of an Army kettle drum drape, of a Signals unit. The panels feature a black Iron Cross edged in silver, and silver National emblem on a deep yellow field. The fringes and tassels are silver. The drape was attached to the kettle drum by means of leather straps.

ABOVE: A detachment of trumpeters at the Berlin Olympics, August, 1936.

BELOW: Fanfare trumpet banners, probably of a Prussian Regiment. Note the music clip on the trumpet.

ABOVE : A late pattern trumpet banner in the form of the Battalion flag. BELOW : A section of a kettle drum drape of non-standard pattern. The background is in the National Tricolour, with a black National Emblem in the centre panel. Silver fringe and tassels.

Charles Scaglione collection

Panzer I and regimental standards on parade as new recruits to a Panzer regiment swear the Oath of Allegiance against the armoured vehicle, as opposed to taking the oath on the Standard as practised by other units. The lower photograph shows in detail the 'swallow tail' regimental standard. Note also the special ribbed pole.

Major John R. Angolia collection

An Army officer's car pennant, double sided. Stretched over a stiff wire frame, the National emblem is embroidered in white and black cotton on a field-grey-coloured base. (All car pennants were contained in a celluloid weather cover, see illustration on page 91.)

Imperial War Museum

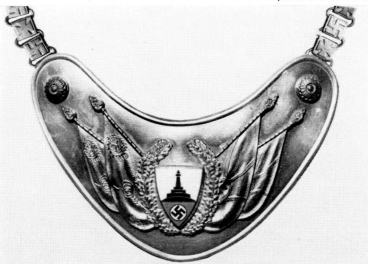

A Veterans' Association (*Reichskriegerbund*) Standard Bearer's gorget, 1st pattern enamel emblem. Polished silver shield, gilt emblems, with red/black/white enamel central device. The chain suspension is gilt metal, and features an alternating design of swastikas and crosses.

Bob Anderson collection

ABOVE: The second pattern Veterans' Association gorget, black/red/silver enamel emblem, otherwise identical to the 1st. This example carries an engraved inscription inside the upper rim, identifying the unit.

Bob Anderson collection

BELOW: A further example of the Veterans' Association gorget, bearing together with an engraved inscription the number 75, denoting the year of foundation of this particular unit. Similar gorgets have been seen to bear 25- and 50-year numerals.

Bob Strodel collection

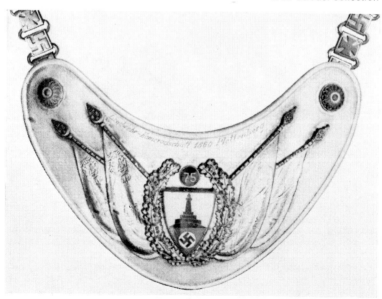

ABOVE: A Veterans' Association member wearing a numbered gorget at an event in Munich, 1939. *Bob Strodel collection*

BELOW AND OVERLEAF TOP: Examples of 25- and 50-year commemorative gorgets.

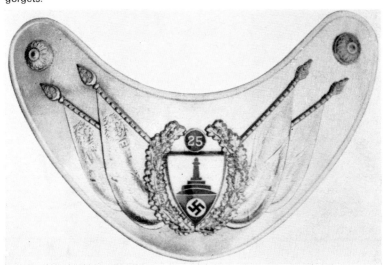

FOLLOWING PAGE, BOTTOM: The NSKOV Standard Bearer's gorget, polished silver finish with gilt emblems, the centre being enamelled in red/white/black. The suspension chain is the same as that of the Veterans' Association gorget. *Bob Anderson collection*

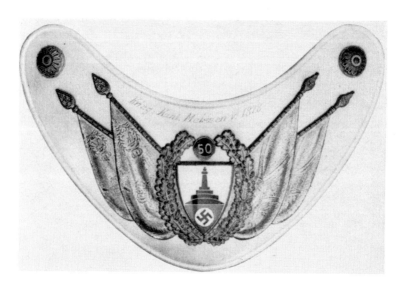

The black Standard of the Saar District NSKOV (National Socialist Disabled War Veterans Association). The flag is here paraded before the Garrison Church at Potsdam, commemorating the return of the Saar Districts to German territory, on March 1, 1935.

Kriegsmarine (Navy)

The flag of a Rear Admiral flying at the masthead of his flagship.

ABOVE: Hitler, accompanied by Generaladmiral Raeder, inspecting Naval personnel with their Standard, following their return from taking part in the occupation of Memel, March 23, 1939.

BOTTOM : Naval Command flags. From left to right they are respectively for an Admiral, Vice-Admiral and Rear Admiral, and were flown from the flagship (or command post ashore) as shown on previous page.

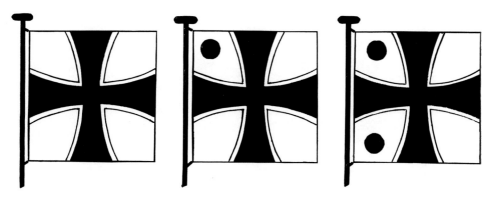

DLV

Dr Christiansen, leader of the DLV (Deutsche Luftsportsverband—German Airsports Organisation) addressing an assembly, most probably at an airfield, sometime in 1935. The DLV national emblem is featured on the rostrum drape, and comprised a black swastika over a silver grey propeller and wings superimposing a white ringed circle on a red field.

BELOW: DLV car pennant.   **Dimensions: 36 cm x 18cm**
                                           Eric Campion collection

NSFK

An NSFK Standard Bearer wearing gorget, and displaying the Standard of Regiment 43.

Major John R. Angolia collection

New Standards being presented by Hitler to NSFK units at Nürnberg, 1937. The NSFK was the National Socialist Flying Corps, a para-military party organisation which gave aviation training and experience, suiting members for Luftwaffe service later. It originally came into being under the name DLV (see page 123) when it functioned to all intents as a Civilian Airsports organisation, there being no Air Training Services in Germany at the time. When the Luftwaffe came into being a high percentage of the DLV membership was transferred directly into the new Service, and the DLV became re-titled NSFK (National Sozialistische Fliegerkorps), now serving purely as a party-sponsored flying organisation.

Luftwaffe
(Air Force)

ABOVE: New recruits to the Spanish Foreign Volunteer 'Blue Division', swearing the Oath of Allegiance on arrival at a Berlin aerodrome, April, 1942. The consecration of the new recruits is symbolised by the crossing of the 'Blue Division' Standard against a Luftwaffe one.

OPPOSITE : A Luftwaffe Regiment receives its Standard. Note that the honour guard and the Standard Bearer carry their swords drawn. The Standard Bearer, an NCO, waits to receive the Standard from the officer who is taking the presentation.

ABOVE : A Guard of Honour of the Luftwaffe Regiment 'General Göring' drawn up in a courtyard of Carinhall, Göring's country estate. The Standards of the Regiment, one of which is shown here, were originally designed for the Police Battalions, the *Landespolizeigruppe General Göring,* which he established in Prussia in 1933. This colour, of the 1st Battalion Standard, was green with a white swastika. The centre was white with a green scroll and black eagle.

Dimensions : 120cm x 120cm

ABOVE: Luftwaffe Standard Bearer's gorget, of matt silver with oxydised silver emblems.

BELOW: The Condor Legion Standard being inspected by Legion members after its presentation. The Condor Legion was the volunteer flying arm sent to Spain during the Civil War. (A colour plate elsewhere in this book shows the same standard in colour.)

ABOVE: Luftwaffe car pennant, woven white and black Luftwaffe eagle on a blue grey ground.

LEFT: A fine bullion Reichmarschall flag, taken from the end of a funeral drape that would have been sent by Göring. The drape would normally comprise two broad ribbons to which would be affixed written condolences made by the sender, and the whole device attached to the wreath sent by, or on behalf of, the Reichsmarschall to the funeral of a dignitary.

Dimensions: 25 cm square, approx.

Eric Campion collection

Göring driving through the streets of Vienna, 1938. Note the Commander-in-Chief of the Air Forces pennant displayed in its transparent rigid frame on the staff car. The pennant is a small-scale version of the large banner shown on the opposite page.

LEFT: The white metal Luftwaffe eagle pike head used with all Luftwaffe standards. It was highly polished and a single casting.

Charles Scaglione collection

Göring was always well known for his flamboyant style of dress, and love of elaborate trappings. The two decorative 'Standards' which were displayed in the entrance hall of his country estate typified this vanity. The banner on the left commemorates his earlier appointment as Prussian Secretary of the Interior, and that on the right his position as Commander-in-Chief of the Air Forces. Colours of the latter were sky blue ground, white diagonals with black borders, gold eagle and wreath, gold and black border and gold fringe.

A section of a Luftwaffe kettle drum drape, featuring a silver bullion eagle on a deep yellow (Signals) background. Silver fringing and tassels. The remaining areas are black.

Charles Scaglione collection

TeNo

Technische Nothilfe (TeNo) was the Technical Emergency Corps, a para-military civilian engineering organisation of volunteers whose function would be to help public authorities in times of emergency.

ABOVE: The Technical Emergency Corps Standard: the field of the flag is white, containing a central red square upon which is superimposed a black swastika and white TeNo emblem.

Illustration courtesy of Dr K. G. Klietmann
Dimensions: 150cm square

BELOW: TeNo Standard Bearer's gorget.

RLB

ABOVE: First Pattern RLB Standard Bearer's gorget.

LEFT: Detail of a first pattern Reichsluftschutzbund (Reich Air Defence) Standard. Silver bullion emblem on a blue/black field.

The Reichsluftschutzbund (RLB)—Reich Air Defence Organisation, was for formed as a civilian-staffed volunteer organisation to render assistance to the Luftwaffe in 1938. It featured a small cadre of full-time personnel, plus a larger contingent of part-time volunteers. During the course of World War 2 the RLB assisted in searchlight control, manning AA guns, fire-spotting etc.